COLUMBIA HOME FRONT WARBOOKS

NUMBER 5

FINANCING TOTAL WAR

By ROBERT MURRAY HAIG

MCVICKAR PROFESSOR OF POLITICAL
ECONOMY, COLUMBIA UNIVERSITY

NEW YORK: MORNINGSIDE HEIGHTS

COLUMBIA UNIVERSITY PRESS
1942

COPYRIGHT 1942

COLUMBIA UNIVERSITY PRESS, NEW YORK

FOREIGN AGENTS: Oxford University Press, Humphrey
Milford, Amen House, London, E. C. 4, England, and
B. I. Building, Nicol Road, Bombay, India

MANUFACTURED IN THE UNITED STATES OF AMERICA

 438

OUR PROGRAM for financing the war is being rapidly hammered out on the anvil of public opinion. In our capacity as citizens, we should be giving earnest consideration to this fundamental question: What kind of program for financing the war ought we to want? The various types of tax and loan and the various types of control, such as rationing and price ceilings, are merely means to an end. The merits of particular methods can be intelligently discussed only after decisions have been reached regarding the objectives to be attained by the general program of war finance.

The war to be financed is a total war. Already it is a total war for our enemies; potentially it is that for us. We are not free to set the pace; it has been set for us. Our foes are determined to win and are throwing into the battle literally everything that will add to the power of their onslaught. Schooled by the experiences of 1914-18, our enemies understand thoroughly the theory and practice of total war; in this struggle, they are fully prepared to accept its uttermost implications.

What are these implications of total war? The most fit must fight; all others must work. Everyone —man, woman, and child—must fight or work, moreover, under direction and to the limit of his endurance. And that endurance is calculated with reference to a short period, with little or no consideration for long-term consequences. Our enemies have shown that for the duration of the war they are prepared to fight and to work to the limit on the basis of a program of consumption that by our accustomed standards is almost unbelievably meager; it is a program carefully designed for maximum short-term efficiency at minimum cost, with practically no leeway for frills and pampering. Total war implies, then, not only a willingness on the part of everyone to fight and to work; it implies also a willingness to sacrifice, a willingness to do without almost everything for the period of the war. For the immediate present, in return for total sacrifice, our enemies can offer their people nothing except a bare living and a pride in playing a part in a magnificent total effort for ends they seem to consider gloriously worth while. For the future they confidently offer them the mastery of the world.

This future reward offered by our enemies to inspire their people to accept the services and sacrifices of total war threatens all that we hold precious in life. Our declaration of war means that we pledge our lives, our property, and our sacred honor to prevent this world from becoming a place in which no one of us would care to live. We have become involved in a total war; we may not like this kind of war, but this is the kind of war we are in. We must prepare ourselves to accept its implications of service and sacrifice to any extent that may prove necessary. If defeat be the alternative, we must be willing to go the extreme limit of sacrifice that has been set by our enemies.

It is only sound sense, of course, for us to seek to keep down to the lowest possible figure these costs of service and sacrifice. Useless and wasteful sacrifice is economic insanity. One difficulty is that at this juncture no one can estimate what the scale of our effort must be in order to win the war. Until victory is clearly in our grasp, we must spare no effort. The best way to insure success, at a minimum aggregate cost, is for us to throw as much as possible into the struggle as quickly as possible. We must do all we can as rapidly as we can and keep on increasing our effort, as we break the successive bottlenecks and overcome the successive limitations that prevent us from making our full force immediately felt. For a time, it was possible to depend largely on idle men and idle plants, but that slack has now largely been taken up. We are now asking our men who were previously busy making automobiles and refrigerators to busy themselves with tanks and planes, and we are doing without new automobiles and refrigerators. We must continue this process of diverting our resources to war purposes until victory is definitely assured. We may hope for victory before the diversion is complete; but we must not count upon it. Perhaps, with good luck, the war will be won before we get into our full stride. But it is possible that, with ill luck, it will be lost because we are unable to strike our full stride soon enough.

Certainly we have started our task under a great handicap in that our enemies were able to organize war economy at their leisure. This task of diverting our resources of men and materials from the ways of peace to the ways of war requires time. It is not accomplished by a mere declaration of war or by the mere passage of a huge appropriation bill by the Congress of the United States. And of time we have pitifully little.

Diversion of our resources to war, diversion at as rapid a rate as possible, and diversion continued at this maximum rate until, if extremity demands it, our full war potential has been translated into military power is the program that lies before us. For the individual, this program of diversion means sacrifice. As the process continues, the amount of sacrifice called for will increase. More and more shall we be forced to accept our pay in something quite different from ordinary consumption goods. If and when we are forced to the extreme limit, we shall reach a point where, as Stephen Leacock has phrased it, everyone will be "working, directly or indirectly, for the conduct of the war and getting nothing, for the moment, but their plain living, and the salvation of their souls."

If this be total war, a plan for financing it should, first and foremost, be one which will facilitate and certainly not retard this process of mobilizing our resources for such a war. As has been pointed out, this process of diversion, this process of beating swords from plowshares, soon involves sacrifice. A good system of war finance should in an equitable manner apportion such sacrifices as may be necessary among the members of the community. It should serve not only to give notice to the community in general as to what aggregate sacrifice of ordinary goods and services is called for during a given time-period, but it should also serve to bring home to each individual in the community a definite indication of what is his proper and equitable share of these sacrifices.

The point has been emphasized that we, as a people, must make available the largest possible amount of goods and services for the prosecution of this war and must make them available as quickly as possible, even though that will mean giving up many goods and services to which we have become accustomed in times of peace. Presently we must turn our attention to the problem of determining how much each of us should give up and the problem of devising methods of making certain that each of us does give up his share. Before doing so, however, it is desirable to analyze this series of questions: Is there not some way of solving the problem that does not involve all this giving-up? Can we not have both guns and butter? Cannot any giving-up that may be involved be done by others than ourselves, perhaps by foreigners, preferably by our enemies? If this is not possible, why should all the sacrifices be asked of this generation? Why not shift them to our children's children?

In terms of physical goods and services, the answers to these questions are not far to seek.

Whatever military strength we may be able to throw into this struggle will have to come primarily from the blood and sweat of this current generation of Americans. We have no great accumulated stocks of munitions; we must make them. For the present, no assistance can be expected from abroad that will reduce our current sacrifices, and probably none can be expected in the future. We cannot wait for future generations to produce either the goods or the services needed. Subject to minor modifications, it may be confidently asserted that whatever efforts and sacrifices may be involved must be supplied by us, here and now.

However, to the extent that we can manage to increase our aggregate product during wartime, a given amount of the war effort need not imply a commensurate reduction of ordinary goods and services. As a matter of fact, we entered upon this war with millions of men unemployed and thousands of machines idle. To the extent that the aggregate product could be increased by putting these men and machines to work at producing the needed goods and services, it was possible, temporarily, to have both guns and butter. Moreover, to the extent that we all work harder and more effectively and to the extent that our wives, our young children, and our aged parents may play a larger role than usual in adding to the aggregate of needed goods and services, to this extent also it will continue to be possible, temporarily, to have both guns and butter.

But let us make haste to state two important qualifications. First, the amount of the added product that can be anticipated from such sources will by no means suffice to provide for the military effort needed. Already in this country we have reached the stage where some butter must be given up. Second, an unemployed man who becomes a munition worker cannot be paid entirely in guns. He will have to take part of his pay in that form, but so will the rest of us. In other words, although the aggregate national heap of goods will grow absolutely, the part of that heap that is butter will decline absolutely and the share of butter than can go to those of us who were employed before the war will have to be reduced in order to enrich the consumption of munitions workers earning forty dollars a week, who before the war were on relief at twenty dollars a week.

It seems clear that in terms of goods and services we must pay for this war ourselves and that this will mean a lot of giving-up of ordinary consumption goods. Moreover, the cost must be met very largely, though not entirely, from current effort; not entirely, because to some extent we can "live on our fat." We can wear out our automobiles and not replace them until after the war; we can kill our cattle for beef and build up our herds after the war; we can allow our houses to go unpainted and allow our machinery to depreciate for lack of costly current upkeep and repairs; we can, systematically, overwork our labor force, either accepting the loss of national productive power involved or counting upon recuperation through future leisure. All such methods throw a burden on the future; but they do not postpone to the future the production of the needed goods and services. Rather, for the benefit of the present, they rob the future of its normal heritage, often at ruinous rates of discount.

If our actual war sacrifices in giving up goods and services to which we have become accustomed can be offset only to a relatively small extent by increased productivity and by using up past accumulations, what are the possibilities of help from outside our national borders? Here it is at once apparent that, in terms of physical goods and services, literally no help is to be anticipated. Everyone knows that we are not on the receiving end of any lease-lend arrangement with our allies. We are on the giving end, for the very good reason that, by increasing our temporary sacrifices for this purpose, there is a rational expectation that our aggregate sacrifices may be minimized by an earlier end of hostilities than would otherwise be possible. Again, we cannot expect to obtain from Germany or Japan in the course of the war any loot that will lessen our current sacrifices.

Let us recall, however, that the preceding questions have been on the level of real goods and services, and in terms of what we must prepare ourselves to give up from our ordinary programs of consumption currently in support of the war effort. That sacrifice must be accepted and borne by us. However, the pattern according to which these current sacrifices are distributed among us in the first instance need not necessarily be identical with the pattern according to which the war sacrifices will be ultimately distributed in the more or less distant future. The present distribution may be tentative in character, subject to future adjustments. Let us illustrate.

Historically, there are instances of wars whose costs to the victors have ultimately been met to a greater or less extent by the vanquished. In this war the sacrifices of the Germans have undoubtedly been lessened by the booty from France and the other subjugated countries of Europe. If Germany should be finally victorious, she would undoubtedly take from us anything we have that she could use, and such spoils of war would compensate to some extent the sacrifices her people have been currently making. During the war of 1914-18 the political leaders of France constantly stimulated their people to sacrifice by promising that a defeated Germany would be compelled to pay all costs. To what a limited extent it proved possible to fulfill these promises is now plainly written on the pages of history. Certainly, prospects of receiving future reparations and indemnities from our beaten and prostrate foes cannot be appraised at a high figure.

Similarly, we shall be well advised if we do not count heavily upon repayments from our allies on lease-lend account. The question of whether we ought to ask for any such repayments need not here be debated. Suffice it to point out that such repayments, if any, would serve as a basis for future offsets for present sacrifices and would tend to make the final pattern of distribution of our sacrifices different from the initial pattern established by current action.

Again, it is possible that the final pattern of real sacrifice may be substantially different from the initial pattern as a result of the use of public credit. This would be the result, for example, if the taxes we levy in the future, to service and repay the defense bonds that we are now selling, should distribute burdens among individuals in a manner substantially different from that in which current bond subscriptions are distributed among our citizens. Suppose, for example, that tomorrow I buy a $1,000 defense bond from savings made by restricting my ordinary consumption by that amount. Suppose further that ten years hence the government levies taxes to pay off its borrowings and I receive $1,000 in redemption of my bond. Suppose finally that my share of those taxes comes to only $500. Clearly the initial pattern of sacrifice as among individuals has been modified in my favor in the final adjustment. Such a modification is both necessary and desirable; the cost of the war should not be finally apportioned in accordance with the willingness of individuals to subscribe to defense bonds.

Note, however, that this does not currently relieve me of the initial sacrifice of giving up the goods and services I would have bought tomorrow with my $1,000 had I not loaned it to the government. This process does not in any real sense transfer the cost of the war to future generations. As a whole, the future generation inherits a debt from the present generation representing sacrifices already made. All that may occur is that the original pattern of sacrifice, drawn according to the willingness of my generation to buy bonds, may be different from the final pattern of sacrifice, drawn according to the liability of a later generation to pay taxes. The task of distributing the burden finally among the members of the group is postponed, but the burden must be assumed by someone, on a tentative basis, when the bonds are originally sold.

To summarize the discussion to this point: Our

plan for financing the war should be, first and foremost, a plan which will facilitate the transformation of our peace economy to a war economy in the shortest possible time. It should be adapted to the economics of total war. As an ultimate limit to which in an extremity we may be forced, literally all of our strength may have to be put into the war effort. We must be prepared to outmatch our enemies in what we *do,* even if that means that we must match them in what we *do without.* Because of the time factor, not all of our strength can be immediately utilized, and pending the date when it can be put to use in the war effort, it may properly be used to produce goods and services which will enrich our ordinary consumption program. During the period in which our economic strength is being diverted to the support of war, the amount by which our standard of living is reduced need not be so great as the amount of the goods and services devoted to the war effort, because the total aggregate productivity of the economy may increase absolutely. This increase may come through the use of men and machines previously idle or less fully or efficiently utilized and by using up, without replacement, our accumulated stocks, our machinery, and our durable consumption goods. However, the great bulk of the goods and services destined for the support of our military endeavor must come from our efforts currently expended and will involve sacrifices in our accustomed standard of living. In the first instance, at least, there is no substantial possibility of shifting these sacrifices to our enemies, to our allies, or to our descendants. We can only shift them about among ourselves. The initial pattern of sacrifice, showing its distribution among individuals, may be modified to some extent by future events and by future action, with the result that the final pattern of sacrifice may be substantially different from the initial one.

We now reach this question: In what manner should the sacrifices involved in this war effort be divided among us? We have said that the distribution of sacrifices should be equitable and fair, but can we agree as to what constitutes equity and fairness?

In trying to answer these questions, consideration is invited to the following three propositions which seem likely to commend themselves to people generally:

1. If there be some who are in a position to benefit economically from the war in a special manner, such persons should, so far as this is technically possible, be asked to surrender those special benefits. In a situation in which citizens in general are called

upon to sacrifice heavily for a common objective, justice requires that none be exempted from sacrifice. Certainly no one should be enriched by a war which impoverishes his country and his fellow citizens.

2. In the final extremity of total war, each of us should be prepared to sacrifice everything he has that may be useful in achieving the objective. In the language of Pigou, in such circumstances "the call from each should be for his *utmost,* rather than for his *share.*"[1]

3. So long as the diversion of resources to the purposes of total war falls short of one hundred percent, so long as the necessity does not exist for each to sacrifice his utmost, the apportionment of sacrifices among individuals should be made in accordance with their relative ability to make sacrifices. Similarly situated individuals should be treated alike, and differentiation among individuals should be in harmony with generally accepted notions of fairness. One such generally accepted notion of fairness is that the call for sacrifices should not be merely proportional to economic strength as tested by property, by income, or by some other criterion; rather, the sacrifices called for may properly increase more rapidly than the absolute

---
[1] A. C. Pigou, *A Study in Public Finance,* 1929, p. 248.

increase in the property or the income of the individual.

It is not proposed to analyze here the justifications that have been advanced in support of the idea of progressive tax rates during the history of the development of economic thought. It is true that these historical justifications have recently been subjected to reëxamination and criticism, but it is noteworthy that the most acute critics of the traditional justifications are the most active workers in the effort to construct new and more sound justifications for progression. It may even be true that the application of the principle of progression in normal times has been pushed to extremes and that the repercussions have been harmful. All this, however, does not impair the validity of the proposition that, under conditions of war, in working out the manner in which the call for sacrifices is to be made, those with large resources should be asked to sacrifice at a greater rate in relation to their resources than those with smaller resources.

The application of these three principles in a particular situation will inevitably give rise to substantial differences of opinion on details. But widespread agreement on these general propositions or on some suitable modification of them should be capable of attainment. Complete agreement in a matter of this sort is of course not to be expected. Compulsion must be resorted to where persuasion fails. But compulsion breeds resentment and resentment prevents full coöperation in the joint enterprise of winning the war. It requires a high order of character to acquiesce cheerfully and not to hold back in the harness, when one's honest opinions regarding equity are not in harmony with those accepted by the community as a whole. Let us hope, however, that such cheerful acquiescence will, in the present hard circumstances, not be lacking.

If for any reason, such as a lack of this cheerful acquiescence or selfish insistence on private interests by special pressure groups, those responsible for the formulation of public policy are forced to make substantial concessions in equity as they formulate their plan of the distribution of wartime sacrifice, serious results in the direction of reduced economic effort are almost inevitable. It is difficult to overemphasize the importance of achieving virtual unanimity of sentiment on this point of what constitutes a fair distribuion of sacrifices in wartime. It is not easy to appeal to a man for hard work and the surrender of a large fraction of the fruits thereof for the common good, if that man has good reason to believe that others are being permitted to escape their fair share of the sacrifices.

It becomes evident, then, that this general answer can be given to the question as to the kind of financing program that we ought to want: we should desire a program that is both adequate and equitable. It should be adequate to the task of facilitating the rapid mobilization of our resources to the support of total war and should ask from us whatever sacrifices may be necessarily involved in that rapid mobilization. It should be equitable in apportioning those sacrifices among us. The plan should not involve us in unnecessary sacrifices and it must not call for administrative skills beyond those which can be made available.

In seeking to perform the mechanical task of apportioning the sacrifices of war among us, a wide range of devices is available, and by no means all of them are fiscal in character.

At one extreme, for example, it is conceivable that the entire economy might be simply drafted, as our sons are drafted for military service. Everyone would be told precisely what he must do and the "plain living" that could be allowed under the war regime would be doled out by a comprehensive rationing system. Fiscal devices would play no role in such a plan. "Constriction of the pantry" could be made effective to any degree considered to be necessary or desirable by nonfiscal controls.

At the other extreme, it is conceivable that complete reliance might be placed upon fiscal devices. "Plain living" would be achieved by "constriction of the pocketbook" through loans and taxes, and the economy would be directed to war purposes, to any degree required, by the use of the government's purchasing power made available to it through those loans and taxes.

With us, the solution of the problem already calls for a judicious mixture of fiscal and nonfiscal devices. Already we have "constriction of the pantry" in the case of certain commodities that are in scarce supply. The need for price control and rationing has already been recognized in the case of a considerable number of articles, and the use of such devices will undoubtedly increase as time advances. It is obvious that the extent to which fiscal devices are called for will depend, in large measure, upon the extent to which it is found necessary and desirable to use nonfiscal controls. Thus the program of war finance is fundamentally conditioned by the program of direct controls that may be adopted. With us, the policy of restricting the use of direct controls to the narrowest limits possible will probably be followed.

It would be intolerably unjust for the government simply to expropriate what it needs without compensation—to ask sacrifices only from those who chance to be in possession of the goods that are needed for waging the war—to seize the Bethlehem Steel Corporation because it can use its products and to leave the Coca-Cola Company alone for the opposite reason. Moreover, such a procedure would be the worst possible method of stimulating the production of war materials.

It has also come to be considered intolerably unjust to ask for sacrifices according to a pattern that results when the government, by some method, direct or indirect, "manufactures money," uses it to buy what it requires, and permits nature to take its course. The inflation of the price level following such a procedure apportions the cost of the war in a manner that does not commend itself to a generation of men which has in its own lifetime had the opportunity to observe and appraise the consequences.

Indeed, the most striking financial phenomenon of the present war is the unanimity with which all the countries, Germany included, have resolved to prevent an inflation of their price levels. With one accord, they appear to have accepted the view that this inflation simply must not be permitted to develop. To prevent its development has come to be a cardinal plank in every plan of war finance. Various types of tax and various types of loan are being examined to ascertain their usefulness for the purpose of checking and controlling inflation and are accepted or rejected largely on the ground of their value for this purpose.

The traditional formula for constructing a program of war finance, and the formula which was followed in the main in financing the war of 1914-18, is roughly the following:

1. Impose as much taxation as you can, giving preference to direct taxes, but also imposing excises and consumption taxes, emphasizing taxes on luxuries.

2. Borrow as much as you can.

3. In the extremity, manufacture your money to any extent necessary.

The result of following this formula was a rise in price levels, very substantial in all the countries involved and disastrously great in the case of several of them.

The danger and undesirability of inflation was recognized during the First World War. However, the analysis of the inflationary possibilities of the various fiscal devices was not carried very far and the problem of forestalling its development, instead of being attacked with vigor, was passed by with an air of pious resignation. The discussion ran in these general terms: If only we can levy enough taxes, we can prevent inflation. There is no hope of doing this, so we must borrow. If we borrow, we shall certainly have inflation. In many cases we cannot even borrow enough to solve our problem, so we must "manufacture money" and try to spend it rapidly enough to keep ahead of the price increases. The attitude at that time is well illustrated by the following passage from Lord Stamp:

Why do governments almost invariably, in war time and afterwards, have to resort to this expedient? First, because most people have to be kept reasonably sweet-tempered (sometimes even the most patriotic), to go on producing hard, and because taxation is psychologically repressive in production. The lessened reward and the smaller fund for reinvestment in new capital have their aggregate effect.

Secondly, because loans also have a definite limit—a limit of credit (in the state) and personal inclination (in the lender). But inflation is easy, and more or less unsuspected and unnoticed while it is going on. If skillfully done, prices creep up, and real rewards in wages and interest are reduced slowly, while business enterprise and employment receive a great fillip.[2]

In other words, inflation is a bunko game. The traditional view has been that this game must be played because people will not face the facts. When

---

[2] Sir Josiah Stamp, *The Financial Aftermath of War*, 1932, pp. 46-47.

they are unwilling to accept their share of the sacrifices, the burden must be slipped to their shoulders by stealth. The people themselves say "yes" to inflation merely by saying "no" to more forthright requests for sacrifice. If inflation is inevitable, the explanation is that the morale of a population at war will not stand the strain of accepting frankly the sacrifices called for by war. However, their refusal to accept the sacrifices frankly does not end the war and the sacrifices have to be accepted anyhow, with interest many times compounded.

In recent decades, the problems of fiscal policy in relationship to the price level have received much attention from economists and the analysis has been carried to new levels. It is now recognized that the situation is much more complicated than was formerly realized. Taxes, we know now, may have inflationary effects. In early 1942 the Federal Reserve Bank of New York felt it necessary to warn the banks against the policy of making loans to individuals to finance the payment of their income taxes, on the grounds that the practice would result in inflation. "To have the volume of purchasing power that is absorbed by taxes replaced on any general scale by extensions of bank credit through individuals borrowing at banks would defeat one of the purposes of higher income taxes . . .

which is the curtailed buying power of consumers."[3]

The sale of government bonds, it is now recognized, need not necessarily have inflationary effects. During the First World War we were urged to "borrow and buy" to the limit. Today we are urged to buy but not borrow. The Defense Bonds that we are offered are nonnegotiable and may not be used as collateral for bank loans. They are designed to absorb purchasing power—to withdraw it from the market. Even normal interest is not paid currently in the case of Series E and Series F bonds, lest it add to the current demand for consumption goods.

The strategy of the current plan for financing the war is so to use the fiscal devices of taxes and loans that effective purchasing power and the available supply of consumers' goods will be kept in such a relationship that inflation of the price level will not occur. The thought is that perhaps we have enough intelligence to be willing to accept our fair share of the sacrifice that this war calls for; that we will not say "yes" to inflation by saying "no" when we are asked to reduce our accustomed program of consumption to the extent called for by the job of diverting our economic effort to war; that we will not,

---
[3] *New York Times*, March 4, 1942.

in the words of the Secretary of the Treasury, "engage in the futile effort to buy more goods than can be produced"[4] while so much of our economy is engaged in making planes and tanks.

Perhaps inflation is inevitable in these United States in this year 1942. We shall soon know. In a remarkable little document (Public Affairs Pamphlet No. 64) that I earnestly urge on your attention, my colleague, John Maurice Clark, in whose judgment on this point I have complete confidence, declares:

We are on the edge of serious inflation. It cannot be prevented by price ceilings alone or by taxes alone, or by credit controls alone. We need all of these, and also an effective policy in the national interest as to farm prices and wages. This last is our most urgent need. . . .[5]

If there is much more buyers' money looking for goods than there are goods looking for buyers, inflation will happen. . . . We must trim the volume of money demand to fit the supply of goods.[6]

This sounds as though the government were planning its taxes to deprive people of goods, but that is not the case. *The requirements of defense have already done that.* What the taxes are for is to save people from wasting their incomes in driving up prices by futile bidding for goods that are not there.[7]

---

[4] *New York Times*, February 4, 1942.
[5] Page 28.
[6] Page 25.
[7] Page 26.

For the first time in the history of the financing of wars, careful estimates are being made as to how much purchasing power will have to be immobilized to avert inflation. My associate, Carl Shoup, has done brilliant pioneering in this field.[8] The fact appears to be that even the tax program laid before the Committee on Ways and Means early in March, 1942, fell substantially short of the necessities of the situation. In the fiscal year 1943 the program, as announced by the President, calls for the expenditure of $59 billion. If one adds $3.0 billion to cover financing of net outlays of certain governmental corporations, new funds to a total of $62.0 billion will be required for the one fiscal year 1943. The recommended changes in taxation, if adopted, will mean that our revenues will amount at most to about $27 billion. Total sales of Defense Bonds (Series E, F, and G) for the ten-month period from May 1, 1941 (when they were first offered) to February 28, 1942, came to the unimpressive total of $4.7 billion,[9] and if this figure can be raised to $12.0 billion for the coming year, an average of a billion a month, the Treasury's fondest expectations will

---

[8] *Federal Finances in the Coming Decade* (Columbia University Press, 1941); also Shoup, Friedman, and Mack, "Amount of Taxes Needed in June, 1942, to Avert Inflation" (mimeographed).

[9] Figures for May to December, 1941, *Treasury Bulletin*, January, 1942; figures for January, 1942, *Federal Reserve Bulletin*, February, 1942; figures for February, 1942, newspaper releases.

apparently be fully realized. Estimates of the total amount of noninflationary borrowing that can be done vary, but $20 billion seems to be generally accepted as coming fairly close to the mark. On this basis, instead of a tax program of $27.0 billion, it would appear that we should be considering a tax program of more than $40.0 billion.

If our leaders are not suggesting a tax program that is adequate to insure against inflation, if they are not yet asking of us what is necessary, if they have not served us with notice of the full amount of the sacrifice that is called for by this total war, what is the explanation of their failure to do so? The answer is plain. Their estimate of our willingness to assume our burdens in this war does not justify them in doing so. We are not being treated as adults. Perhaps we do not deserve to be treated as adults. As I read my newspaper, I am not confident that we do deserve to be treated as adults. Many of us seem to be concerned exclusively with the futile task of attempting to insure that none of the sacrifices of the war shall fall on any one of us. As yet we seem not to have faced the realities of our situation. We must work together to increase production to the utmost and at the same time we must be willing to give up for the present a very large part of what we normally consume. If each of us, upon threats of withholding productive effort, insists upon a smaller share of the sacrifices than is equitable by accepted community standards, we cannot hope to match the pace that is being set for us by our enemies.

At the present moment—March 5, 1942—a war revenue act is being prepared. Most of the specific questions being discussed stem from this failure to face the realities of the situation. Our leaders fear that as a group we are unwilling to accept the burden of taxation that is really called for. All parties in interest—the workers, the farmers, the investors, the business and financial leaders—insist upon a different pattern for distributing the inevitable sacrifices of the war. Every objection carries an implied threat to withhold productive effort that is vital to the achievement of the task of mobilizing all our resources for war at the earliest possible moment. The time has arrived when we must recognize the necessity for sacrifice by us all and the necessity for agreeing upon a basis for its distribution. Jockeying to shift the burden about among ourselves, under threats to withhold productive effort, may easily proceed to a point where it will seriously impair our power to make war.

In view of these facts, no apology is offered for attempting here to focus attention primarily upon the question as to what we should try to accomplish by our various fiscal devices rather than upon the relative merits of different types of tax and loan. The plain fact is that the foundations of the program of war finance are more important than the superstructure. Once we arrive at a general agreement as to the ends for which we should strive, once we secure a general recognition of the supreme importance of those ends, and once we achieve general acceptance of the principles that should control the apportionment of sacrifice, the task of formulating a detailed program tends to become a technical problem of writing a formula. The structure of war finance must in this democratic state be reared on a foundation of willing hearts—the hearts of the great body of its citizens who understand the fundamental character of the issues at stake, citizens who recognize the vital importance of the objectives, citizens who are convinced of the necessity for the great sacrifices required, citizens who have brought themselves to agree upon the tests to be used in apportioning those sacrifices and who are prepared to submerge their individual and group interests and to coöperate with all their might in a joint endeavor for the common good. The implications for each of us are clear. Let us see to it that what needs to be done in financing this war shall not fail to be done because we are unwilling to make the sacrifices called for by that program. May the morale of the American at War be equal to the task of financing this war as it should, in the general interest, be financed!

Bei Fragen zur Produktsicherheit wenden Sie sich bitte an:
If you have any questions regarding product safety,
please contact:

Walter de Gruyter GmbH
Genthiner Straße 13
10785 Berlin
productsafety@degruyterbrill.com